8 STEPS TO BE A CHAMPION

by WALTER SCOTT

TO: ───────────────────────────

FROM: ─────────────────────────

DATE ──────────────────────────

Published by EPIC Press

Published by EPIC PRESS

Copyright 2016 Champion Basketball Training

All rights reserved worldwide. No part of this book may be reproduced or transmitted in any form or by any means electronic or mechanical, including photocopying, recording or by any information storage and retrieval system without written permission from Walter Scott and Champion Basketball Training.

Printed in the United States of America

ISBN: 978-1523814725

1. Leadership 2. Sports Champion Basketball Training: 8 Steps To Become A Champion

Disclaimer/Warning:

This book is intended for lecture and entertainment purposes only. The author or publisher does not guarantee that anyone following these steps will be a successful leader. The author and publisher shall have neither liability responsibility to anyone with respect to any loss or damage cause, or alleged to be caused, directly or indirectly by the information contained in this book.

TABLE OF CONTENTS

Introduction 9

Chapter 1 - Courage 12

Chapter 2 - Heart 18

Chapter 3 - Adversity 23

Chapter 4 - Mentality 29

Chapter 5 - Preparation 36

Chapter 6 - Inspiration 42

Chapter 7 - Opportunity 46

Chapter 8 - Never Give Up 52

8 Steps of Becoming a Champion Guide 59

Goal Sheets 68

ACKNOWLEDGEMENTS

My family provides me with the support and stability to passionately strive to impact and empower as many youth and people of all walks of life as possible to be Champions. First and foremost I have to thank my beautiful wife of 11 years Cassandra for the love and support she has shown me over the years. I can't thank her enough for trusting that everything would work out fine when I decided to resign from my financial sales job in 2008 and embark on my journey as an entrepreneur.

Next, I have to acknowledge my two wonderful kids Brynne and Parker Scott. Observing their precious faces and being around their brilliance and fun loving spirits challenges me every day to become the best person I can be and provide them with the best life possible. Although it is too early for names, I want to acknowledge our newest Scott addition that is scheduled to arrive in June of 2017.

I must thank my parents Herbert and Minnie Scott for all the lessons they taught me growing up. The morals and ethics I govern my life by were shaped by what was instilled in me through their parenting. I'll be forever grateful for their love and

Acknowledgements

support along with my brothers Herbert and Richard Scott and sister Minniequa Scott. Other family members I would like to thank are my sister in law Sherrie Scott, my mother in law Paula Williams and brother and sister in law Christian and Sarah Williams for their support.

Now I must transition and give thanks to the individuals who had confidence and believed in me professionally. I'm so grateful for these awesome groups of parents:

Stacey Bowe, Shayla Lewis, Jennifer Hicks, Michelle Dusek, Shannon Wheeler, Kimberly Johnston, Anthony Blacknall, Shannon Nichol, Wendy Blackburn, Wendy Hattaway, Dustin Smith, Nannette Mulkey, Amy Wade, Jennifer Reever, Jennifer Hill, Jennifer Tenney, Christy Lee, Mark Busby, LaVonda Vestal, Jennifer Chaney, Salvador Lozoya, Melanie Green....

These parents support made it clear that they valued the coaching I provided their kids. Their continued support throughout the years energized and inspired me to be laser focused and provide the greatest impact possible when in the presence of all youth.

So much of this book involves players that I trained and coached. How could I not thank them as well as many players who were not mentioned for the experiences as well as the knowledge they have contributed to this book?

Special thanks go to Coach Douglas who gave me my first opportunity to run a camp in Lone Oak back in 2009. Also, I want to thank Marc McCartney for camps he assisted me in running as well other coaches who were instrumental in the early days of my training career.

When a book project crosses the finish line, it's all too easy to forget how it all began, and I can't let that happen. Prior to him becoming my business coach I reached out to Darren Palmer and asked him for some tips to gain clarity about writing my story. He has since then become my business coach and leant his expertise and resources to guide me through the book writing process and for that I am forever grateful. Darren has made such an impact on me not only as professional but as a person. Not only have I gained a valuable business coach, but also a brother. I also have EPIC Publishing to thank for the awesome job taking my story and making it into this fabulous book and bringing it to the readers.

INTRODUCTION

Growth is an essential part of personal development. If there's one thing on which I'm an authority, it's how to bring the best out of others and empower them to realize for themselves they are capable of achieving more. My strong belief is this: Showing someone who they are will guide them in becoming who they are capable of becoming.

This book is about developing the behaviors and mindsets not only to be successful at reaching goals and dreams but also becoming the best version of YOU. It will give you the tools to be successful in all your future endeavors.

To this point, I've had a rewarding and fulfilling career helping youth become successful on the court and in life. Some of the success stories of my trainees will be shared in this book. Stories of triumph, perseverance, breaking through comfort zones and barriers and never settling for less than reaching their full potential. All of them have a purpose: to help you pave your own personal pathway to greatness, whatever you do in life.

During my career I have witnessed season after season, parents fill the stands game after game with the desire for their son or daughter to be successful. In turn, their athlete's performance on the court brings them satisfaction.

As a basketball trainer who is also a parent, I understand this desire, but I ask this question - Is scoring points, getting rebounds, making assists, or even the final score enough? My 8 years of experience as a trainer has made it crystal clear to me how players feel about themselves determine how they perform.

As great a feeling as it is for basketball players to achieve success on the court, who they become in the process is most vital. Achievement on the court only lasts for a particular season, but the payoff of developing the mindset and behaviors of a Champion last a lifetime.

This understanding leads me to give players and parents the necessary tools to equip athletes to reach a higher pinnacle of success that comes with becoming a Champion. Before we discover what it takes to be a Champion, let's first recognize that the most critical step in an athlete's success is goal setting. How can a player expect success during basketball season if they don't first sit down and develop their blueprint for the hardwood?

Goal setting should be multi-dimensional:

- Individual goals for practice
- Goals for each game (i.e., how many points, assists, rebounds, etc.)
- Goals for the season to include any honors they wish to achieve (i.e., All-District, All-State, etc.)

Goal setting is critical, allowing players targets to strive for, but also a way to measure their progress throughout the season. I will further discuss the importance of goal setting in the preparation chapter of this book.

Now that we have decided what we desire for our game by game success and more importantly, our season, let's discover how to make our goals become a reality using the C.H.A.M.P.I.O.N. method.

Chapter 1

COURAGE

> *It takes courage to grow up and become who you really are"*
>
> – e.e. cummings

Courage

Courage requires us to make a choice when we don't know what is on the other side of this decision. We are only truly courageous when we proceed to pursue our goals despite the uncertainty of knowing how things will turn out. All worthwhile accomplishments begin with courage. The most important accomplishment, which is players reaching their full potential, requires courage.

Those striving to be champions are most challenged by goals that are far-fetched. The true measure of courage is giving maximum energy and effort while being truly committed when you are unsure of the outcome. Somehow, miracles happen when individuals decide to go after their dreams and goals even if they are not sure of the outcome. Miracles? What? Let me tell you how.

On February 21, 2013, just a few days after Haley Trentham had played her last high school game as a Celeste Blue Devil, she was nervous about whether or not her dream of playing college basketball would come true. Haley and I spent a lot of time during her high school career working on her basketball skills, which resulted in her becoming a poised point guard with excellent ball-handling abilities and a nice jump shot to go along with her high basketball IQ and her ability to make her teammates better. However, despite Haley being a phenomenal high school player, her 5'4" frame was considered small by college standards and to top it off, Haley lacked the lightning speed that allows smaller guards the opportunity to catch the eye of college coaches. Also, playing at a 1A high school, even though it was a State Championship powerhouse in the 90's, limited her chances of being on any college coach's radar.

With the odds stacked against her, Haley activated the power of courage when she reached out to me and declared, "Walter, I really want to play college basketball," even though she had no clue whether it was even possible. My response to Haley was, "Haley, if you want something bad enough, you don't have to know how it's going to happen. Just believe strongly enough that it can happen." With no prospects of colleges to play for, we got to the gym and worked tirelessly for the next 3 weeks. During this time, an opportunity to play in a High School All-Star game came about. A college basketball tryout also surfaced.

Haley had fun during the All-Star game. Her skills were sharp, and she played well as a result of the work she put in preparing for the game.

Haley's performance against the best high school players in the area gave her confidence going into her tryout at Tarleton State University. Upon arrival at the tryout, Haley had no idea what to expect. All she could rely on was the prior 3 weeks spent sharpening her skills and the years of training and playing high school and AAU ball. As it turned out, all of Haley's preparation paid dividends, resulting in her performing well during the tryout. Haley received word a couple of weeks later that she had made the team. With that, Haley accomplished what she had dreamed about for years when she officially signed with Tarleton State on May 8, 2013.

Like Haley, we can also achieve our goals and dreams. Even the far-fetched ones. All by conquering the 4 stages of courage.

4 STAGES OF COURAGE

1. Decide what you want to achieve.
2. Decide to get started and begin to take steps toward reaching your goals and dreams.
3. Continually put in the work that is required to reach your goals without allowing yourself to be sabotaged by the voice of fear that will surface from your mind. This voice will attempt to convince you that you are not capable and cause you to question whether you have what it takes to accomplish your goal.
4. Be patient with the process. Resist the urge to rush the process and continue to work until your goal becomes reality.

Haley reaching her goal of putting on a Tarleton State jersey and going to her first practice and playing in her first game was possible only because she believed it was possible while demonstrating courage. Just like Haley, courage is just the first step for you to become the star basketball player you wish to become, but it is also a gateway to becoming a Champion. You now have a decision to make now that you know what courage is and how important it is: Will you become courageous and go after your dreams and goals wholeheartedly to accomplish them or will you become impatient and discouraged eventually giving up on your goals?

BREAKTIME

At the end of each chapter, we will take a break and recap where 8 Steps to Becoming a Champion has taken us up until this point.

(Step 1: Be Courageous)

So far, we've learned that exercising courage is how we make our dreams and goals come true. In order to reach our goals, we must first determine what we want to accomplish, then have the courage to take the necessary steps and continue to be courageous until our goals are reached.

Chapter 2

HEART

> *It's not about talent. It's about Heart. It's about who can go out there and play the hardest. They aren't gonna give you anything. You go out there and take it."*

– Glory Road

HEART

An athlete who loves to compete has Heart. Heart is what gives Champions the slight edge. To help us better understand what it means to have Heart let's look at the two distinct ways that define

Heart:

1. First is the ability to tap into what really motivates you
2. Second is the ability to dig deeper and find a little extra energy and effort at pivotal times.

TRAINER'S TIP

Write down 3 reasons why it is important for you to reach your desired goals and dreams?

(Constantly remind yourself of these three reasons when things are most difficult.)

Although it is hard to measure heart, it is a force to be reckoned with nonetheless. What drives some players to achieve great things on the basketball court simply comes down to the eagerness to compete and love for the game. Let's learn from

Haley Hicks how circumstances change when you go beyond talent and skill and activate Heart.

Haley worked and prepared for years to be a Lady Jacket. So beginning her sophomore season on Varsity with players she formerly looked up to had Haley more than excited. Haley was eager to learn her coaches' expectations, and she worked hard during practice getting acclimated to the Varsity level. It was surreal for Haley to finally be running out in the same Lady Jacket uniform that she had watched great players before her wear. Unfortunately, the newness wore off, and some excitement began to wane because the 2014-2015 team was loaded with Seniors which meant zero playing time through the first 6 games with no sight of future playing time. Sitting on the bench and just watching was hard for Haley due to her love for the game and her competitive drive. I remember having a conversation with Haley during this time. I told Haley that it was hard work that got her to Varsity as a Sophomore and it would be hard work that would get her playing time. Haley began to dig deep and operate from HEART by being the first person to morning practices, staying after practice, and coming to the gym on weekends. I also informed Haley during this time that if she worked harder and prepared more, that more opportunities would present themselves. Haley was given an opportunity to play for a few minutes later in the season, and that small opportunity turned into a lot more playing time because of the 3-point shooting she displayed during that brief opportunity. Not only did Haley end up having a stellar Sophomore year and an even greater Junior year finishing ranked #7 in DFW in 3-Pointers made for all of 6A. Moreover, Haley also received First Team All -District honors all because of her having HEART.

The biggest part of winning and being successful is making a decision. You can reach any goal you desire by deciding to implement the following steps whenever you have very challenging goals and dreams.

2 STEPS TO TRIGGER HEART

1. Have big enough reasons why you must reach your goal or dream?
2. Visualize what it would look like and feel like to reach your goal or dream.

Achieving greatness is attainable if you are able to dig deeper when things are difficult and uncertain. The challenge is not understanding what it means to have heart, but instead, will you find the inner strength to put in the necessary work until the desired outcome is accomplished and you become a Champion in the process?

BREAKTIME

(Step 2: Tap into your HEART)

Let's recap. To accomplish anything of significance trials and tribulations are a part of the process, therefore having HEART will give you the inner strength to continue working despite fatigue or doubt. Heart is what gives you the slight edge and qualifies you to become a CHAMPION.

Chapter 3

ADVERSITY

A champion is defined by the adversity he overcomes."

– Anderson Silva

Adversity is obstacles and challenges you'll face during the journey to reaching your goals and dreams. Understanding the theory of adversity is not as much the challenge as actually dealing with it. The biggest challenge when encountering adversity is that it's often times unexpected; therefore, there is no way to plan for it in advance. Let me tell you how the adversity I faced became the defining moment of my training career.

Looking back and reflecting, it's hard to believe that if I hadn't persevered, I never would have had the opportunity to train and empower Haley Trentham, Haley Hicks, or many other players to achieve extraordinary success on the court. It was March of 2008 and with marketing material in hand, I set out to secure gym space to begin my dream of helping local players become more skilled basketball players. After weeks turned into months, and I still had no luck finding a gym for training, I realized that in all of my planning, I didn't plan on not having a location to train. How I decided to proceed during this adverse situation determined my fate as a trainer. Believing in the VISION so strongly is what gave me the courage to proceed. My thoughts began to be that I would pursue my dreams no matter what. At this moment, I realized

ADVERSITY

I had a basketball goal in my front yard and had local parks available to me. I used what resources were available at the time and although they were very humble beginnings, my dream and goals as a skills trainer had begun.

TRAINER'S TIP

Be faithful over a few things, and he will make you manager over many.

Matthew 25:23

Miracle Territory resides just beyond adverse situations

Because I decided I would not surrender and was determined to pursue my dream no matter the circumstances life rewarded me with some pivotal opportunities. Haley Trentham was one of my first clients whose parents supported and valued the training even though it was outdoors and sometimes in 100 degrees Texas heat. Haley's rapid improvement and early success along with a few other clients at the time led to word of mouth and finally the opportunity to get indoors and train. I'm so thankful that 8 years later I have trained thousands of players in many different gyms. Furthermore, because I persevered despite adversity, I was able not only to reveal to myself but the world my true authentic self and discover my gift of empowering and motivating others to reach their full potential. Not to mention also accomplishing great feats such as writing this book.

Champions are measured by their ability to overcome adversity

On your journey to success, just know that adversity is inevitable. It is a part of the process. When you encounter adverse situations they reveal whether you have what it takes to be a winner. Furthermore, the significance of your dreams must empower you to embrace your adverse situation and face it head on. The ability to be mentally tough while overcoming adversity is what separates the Champions from contenders.

CHAMPION STEPS TO OVERCOMING ADVERSITY

Be a CHAMPION and recognize adversity and overcome it by following these steps:

1. Focus on what you can control
2. Remind yourself that there is nothing else you would rather do than reach your goals and dreams
3. Analyze your situation and determine steps you can take to become better and get closer to your goals and dreams

In closing, it's not what happens to you, but how you respond to it. In the face of adversity, you have 3 choices:

You can let it define who you are

Or

You can be destroyed by it

Or

You can be strengthened by it.

BREAK TIME

(Step 3: Overcome Adversity)

It's recap time. We've learned that we shouldn't be surprised by adversity, but expect it. Most importantly, we should now understand that how we handle adversity separates us from our competitors and defines us as champions.

Chapter 4

MENTALITY

You are always responsible for how you act, no matter how you feel."

– Robert Tew

Winning and losing begins with our thinking. Actions we take are dictated by what we think and how we think. Winners expect to win; therefore, they think like winners. Moreover, one slight difference between a champion and non-champion oftentimes boils down to mentality. When some give up and give in, Champions maintain the mindset to give 100% effort and energy despite circumstances and situations. In order to have the mentality of a champion, your expectations and thinking must be in agreement. The reality is as a player your performance can't rise above how you view yourself. Having a champion's mentality can determine whether you reach your full potential, but the alternative will lead you to settle for less than you are capable of. Let's learn from Brady Mulkey why we must do whatever it takes to reach our dreams and goals.

Brady Mulkey was a late bloomer who really started to develop into a college prospect during the summer of his junior year going into his senior season. At 6'7", Brady was undersized by college standards. Therefore, he had to transition from a position he had played all of his life, Forward/Center, and develop into a wing player in order to have a chance at playing college basketball. Needless to say, change is hard and often times takes a lot of hours and hard work. During Brady's entire junior year, he and I spent hours working on his ball handling, midrange shooting, and 3 point shooting. Brady began to adapt to playing the perimeter and began being a player his coach could count on for scoring and rebounding. The challenge was that Brady's high school team had a bad 2nd half of the season during his junior year and the losing spilled over into his senior season. Although Brady had developed into a college prospect by this time, not being part of a winning program and lacking visibility resulted in him not being on college coaches' radars. Fortunately, by the end of the season, Brady was able to pique the interest of a couple of D3 coaches. Division 3 was not Brady's ideal scenario, but he visited a couple of campuses anyway and even caught a D3 game. While watching the D3 contest, Brady couldn't get past the feeling that he wasn't satisfied with his present options. Brady decided he was not going to settle for playing at the D3 level instead he chose to follow his heart of at least playing at the Division 2 level. Brady proceeded to play AAU ball as an unsigned senior.

Brady was fortunate to join a very competitive AAU team whose coach had a great reputation and rapport with college coaches. The challenge Brady now faced was adjusting to the speed of the game with and against other college-caliber players. The AAU season was going well, but still no offers. As the final tournaments approached, Brady started to realize it was do or die time. As this realization started to sink in, Brady's mentality began to be, "I'm going to lay it all on the line and leave it all on the court and play as if there were no tomorrow." As fate would have it, scouts from Division 2 Southern Nazarene University were present and were interested in signing Brady to a scholarship offer. Due to his never wavering during the process, Brady is now preparing for his College Sophomore basketball season at SNU all because of his champion mentality to not settle and do whatever it took to reach his goals and dreams.

How serious are you about realizing your goals and dreams? Don't just be someone who hopes and wishes they could reach their goals and dreams. Before you continue, be completely honest and ask yourself these three questions to determine your mentality:

- Am I giving 100% effort and energy despite the situation and circumstances?
- Do I truly expect to reach the goals and dreams that I have written down?
- Am I pursuing my goals and going the extra mile, especially when things seem to be the hardest and most uncertain?

Because being a champion has less to do with talent and ability and more to do with mentality, it's within your reach if you are willing to think like a champion and take necessary steps to do whatever it takes and work as hard and as long as needed to be victorious.

CHAMPION CREED

I have the **C**ourage to

I have enough **H**eart to

I constantly overcome **A**dversity in order to

I'm equipped with the **M**entality to

Every day I wake and **P**repare to

I find the necessary **I**nspiration to

I take advantage of **O**pportunities to

I have decided I will **N**ever Give Up until I

WIN

BREAKTIME

(Step 4: Be equipped with winners MENTALITY)

It's time to recap what we've learned. We learned that winning and losing begins with our thinking. Our dominant thoughts show up in our performance. If we expect to win and think like winners, as a result we perform like winners. Therefore, inevitably we experience victory and are well on our way to becoming Champions.

Chapter 5

PREPARATION

❝

Success is where preparation and opportunity meet."

– Bobby Unser

Preparation

Preparation allows you to get ready for the game before the game. Preparation is the most important thing any player can do. Winning and losing often come down to how much or how little an individual or team prepares. This is where champions separate themselves because many will not go through the repetitive, non-glamourous, unimpressive work to improve their game. During your preparation, you can't forget your Winner's mentality. Because you expect to win, you must not just prepare, you must prepare to win. As champions, how you prepare is very important because the results you get during performance are a byproduct of the quality or lack thereof during your practice time. Furthermore, as a champion, it is important to make sure your level of preparation matches your level of expected play. I've trained many successful players during my career, but few who prepared for competition as much as Kimmy Blackburn did.

Prior to me working with Kimmy, she already had success during her Freshman through Junior years, leading her team in all statistical categories and helping her team reach the playoffs each season, so clearly Kimmy was the star of her high school team. The motivation for Kimmy's parents reaching out to me was to prepare her for college basketball and to help her get in position to play at the college level. I began working with Kimmy during the summer leading into her senior year. My question to her was, "What are the goals you wish to accomplish this season?" Kimmy stated that she wanted to be district MVP, which she hadn't accomplished yet during her high school career. Now that we had established what we were setting out to accomplish, it was time to get to work. We began working on making Kimmy better at her strengths, but also on improving her weaknesses. All the off-season training was ball handling, offensive moves and conditioning, so Kimmy would be prepared for the start of the season. Where Kimmy gained separation from the competition truly happened during the season. We found every possible opportunity to get in the gym and put in the extra work. On Saturday mornings right after Friday night games, a couple hours before tournament games, Sunday morning before church, in addition to our weekly skill training sessions. As a result of all the hard work, Kimmy had a phenomenal Senior season being named All-Tournament, All-Texoma, District MVP, and even better, she was named to the TABC All-Region selection. Kimmy is now looking to continue her basketball success at the college level as she enters her sophomore season at The University of Texas at Tyler.

Just as we learned from Kimmy, preparation might not always be easy, but it gives you a competitive advantage because not everyone is going to put in the extra work. Preparation is hard work, but with it comes rewards.

BENEFITS OF PREPARATION

- Leads to confidence
- Improvements to skills
- Competitive advantage over your competition
- Proper preparation always pays off. You're guaranteed to get the results during performance equal to the quality of your preparation time.
- Builds muscle memory which allows you to perform skills without much thought allowing you to focus on thinking the game and playing the game off of feel, reaction, and instinct

HOW YOU PREPARE IMPACTS YOUR LEVEL OF SUCCESS

We have covered in great detail the importance and value of preparation. I believe it is just as important to have a preparation plan. Now is a great time to revisit setting preparation goals as I mentioned in the introduction of the book. I recommend players set daily goals in which you set individual goals for team practice, such as give 100% during practice, give the coach undivided attention during the entire practice, be a leader and lead by example, learn plays quickly and perform coaches' expectations with excellence. Moreover, players set daily goals for outside practice, i.e., 10 minutes of ball-handling, make 25 shots from perimeter, jump rope routine, etc.

In closing, champions don't practice on their opportunities, they instead put in numerous of hours of preparation no one ever sees. Moreover, they are willing to accept delayed gratification for future payoff. Now that you have the blueprint to prepare like a champion, the question is, will you get in the gym and put in the extra work?

BREAKTIME

(Step 5: Prepare to win)

It's recap time again. We were taught that preparation is the most important thing we can do. Moreover, we must prepare to win and make sure our preparation matches our level of expected performance.

Chapter 6

INSPIRATION

❝

You were born to be a player. You were meant to be here. This moment is yours."

– Herb Brooks

Inspiration

Inspiration is an energy source and motivational agent that makes players strive to reach their greatness. Part of being successful is staying inspired. It's paramount to stay inspired by what you envision for yourself, instead of focusing so much on the present reality. What you see happening in your mind, will have to happen in time. To be good at the game of basketball, not to mention great, requires a lot of hard work. Often times when you are tired and fatigued, your mind attempts to convince you to stay in your comfort zone. Instead of falling into the comfort zone trap, find a source of inspiration that motivates you to go a little further and take a few more steps toward your goals and dreams. Inspiration also serves as a catalyst to aid you in staying focused on going after what you truly want to accomplish and not settle. Being the person putting my trainees through the grueling tough workouts, I know the hard work they put in. During training, my work is more mental as I instruct; therefore, I exert minimal physical energy. Because of this fact, there could be a misconception about how physically grueling my job really is. If the truth be told, there is a ton of behind the scenes work I do daily. My daily routine consists of 1-2 hours of ball handling, 30 minutes-1 hour working on specific moves, and 20-30 minutes running. There are definitely days I do not feel up to putting in preparation time. On these days specifically, I find inspiration thinking about my trainees and how can I empower them to be champions unless I'm a champion first? My truest inspiration comes from seeing young people reach their goals. Because of this fact, I constantly draw on this inspiration to become better daily so I can, in turn, help players reach their full potential. I have no interest in taking full credit for success that my trainees experience because they put in the work. But, I do enjoy the feeling of playing a small role in them seeing who they are capable of becoming. There is no greater inspiration than knowing I am using my God-Given gift of inspiring and empowering youth to be successful through the game of basketball.

What individual(s) do you most admire? And does their story inspire you to become better as a player and person? When you are working toward your goals and dreams how often do you think about how proud your loved ones will be when you are successful?

INSPIRATION IS KEY TO YOUR SUCCESS

Whatever your goal might be-making the varsity team, being a starter on your varsity team, being the leading scorer, or even playing college basketball, none of these things will be given to you. Not only will hard work and dedication be required, but also inspiration to keep you going when the journey becomes difficult and hard times occur.

In closing, don't just show up to practice or a game, but constantly spend time reconnecting to your inspirational sources. There is more at stake here than just the outcome of the game. It's about who you become in the process. You've come too far not to become a Champion.

BREAKTIME

(Step 6: Stay Inspired)

It's recap time. We learned that part of being successful is staying inspired. Avoid the comfort zone trap by finding sources of inspiration that motivate you to continue taking necessary steps until you achieve your goals and dreams.

Chapter 7

OPPORTUNITY

❝

Some people want it to happen, some wish it would happen, others make it happen."

– Michael Jordan

Opportunity

Who would pass up a chance to do something they felt to be rewarding or beneficial? There is not more that you can ask for than an opportunity, especially when it revolves around something you like, enjoy, and are passionate about. Having the opportunity to play the game you enjoy is one thing, but Champions understand taking full advantage of opportunities is more important than just having them. Moreover, opportunities should be taken advantage of even when they cause you to be fearful, and they present themselves during uncertain times. Pay close attention as Lexi and Jayla Hattaway teach us how opportunities can drastically change your high school basketball career.

Lexi and Jayla transferred schools toward the end of their Sophomore year, and understandably so they were unsure what the future held in their new environment. In the mean time they geared up to play summer ball on a select team I assisted in coaching. Lexi's adjusting to the summer team was affected by the opportunity to play primary as a guard which was out of her comfort zone. Lexi played forward only her first two seasons of high school basketball. Jayla's fear of the opportunity to play select ball was due to her lack of playing time during her sophomore season, and also she was under the impression that the players she would be playing against in tournaments were so much better than she was. They both experienced growing pains but eventually welcomed the challenge. I was able to finally convince Lexi that she was talented enough and perfectly capable to transition from forward to guard. Also, Jayla bought into the fact that as coaches we would definitely put her in situations to succeed. After a few tournaments under their belt, both players began to really flourish and grow as basketball players. Lexi became our most versatile player being able to handle the ball, rebound, drive to the basket and also knock down 3-Pointers as well as be a good defender. Jayla's ball handling ability started to shine through paired with her blazing speed resulting in her having a new found level of success. As awesome as it was seeing these two wonderful young ladies be successful during summer ball the real benefit came once they began their high school junior season. Now that Lexi and Jayla were scheduled to suit up for the Lady Wolves excitement began to brew. Jayla and Lexi did not disappoint. Jayla was now settling in as starting point guard and leading the team while Lexi was doing what she does as Ms. Versatile. They both had a tremendous impact on the team so much so that Wolfe City Lady Wolves went from last place in the district in 2014-15 to tie for 1st place at season end of 2015-16 season. Even more exciting was the fact that Jayla and Lexi's stellar play and leadership spearheaded Wolfe City girls basketball team to the playoffs for the first time in 20 yrs. Unfortunately, their playoff run was cut short when they faced defending State Champions Martin's Mill during the area round of the playoffs. Nevertheless, the memories and impact they made on the Wolfe City program will be remembered for a long time. With a strong senior season, they will definitely leave a legacy at Wolfe City that will not be soon forgotten. These ladies showed us how great things can be accomplished when Champions take full advantage of opportunities.

TAKE FULL ADVANTAGE OF OPPORTUNITIES

Champions rise up and take full advantage of opportunities and not shy away from them. The significance of an opportunity can't stop at being excited about a chance to do something you enjoy. What allows you as a Champion to separate from your competition is you considering the responsibility that comes with your opportunities and make sure you are prepared for them as well. As you prepare for your next season I would like you to periodically ask yourself these questions:

1. Am I starting practice with the mindset of getting better?
2. How am I making sure I'm as prepared for upcoming games as much as possible and not just relying on coach to make sure I'm prepared?
3. Do I make my teammates better?
4. Is my team better because I'm on the team and why?
5. What things will I commit to doing each week to make my team better?

TRAINER'S TIP

- Practice is most important opportunity
- Practice is more important than the game
- Coaches gain confidence in players during practice

In closing seize every opportunity you are given to get better. Give your best effort every time you step on the basketball court whether it be practice or games. The reality is your future opportunities depend on how you manage your current ones.

BREAK TIME

(Step 7: Take advantage of every OPPORTUNITY)

Taking full advantage of opportunities is more important than just having them. As a Champion, you separate from the competition by considering the responsibility that comes with your opportunities and make sure you are prepared for them as well.

Chapter 8

NEVER GIVE UP

"

Don't quit. Suffer now and live the rest of your life as a Champion"

– Muhammad Ali

Throughout the book, I wanted to incorporate the stories of some of my former trainees to make the principles of becoming a Champion more impactful. Including some of my players' stories was important because without them this particular book would not be possible. However, I thought it is only fitting that I share more of my story because Never Giving Up is the only reason I have progressed to this point in my career and have had experiences that equipped me to motivate and empower you to become successful. If you have a goal or dream that is constantly in your mind and heart, you must pursue it and never give up on it. Let me share with you how pursuing my goal changed my life forever.

It was February 2008, and I had resigned from my Financial Sales job. During this time, I was unsure of what my next move would be. Suddenly I became led to try and fulfill one of my prior goals I had written down months or even years before starting my own business. Watching local basketball games, I saw a need for helping youth players develop their basketball skills. I spent time coming up with a brochure, i.e., my vision on paper and began on my journey of helping young people be more successful at the game of basketball. As

I stated in Chapter 3, the pivotal moment for my training career was not being derailed because I didn't have gym space to train when I first started out. Deciding to use the goal in my front yard and parks for training was a solution for the first hurdle. My next hurdle was just as daunting. I remember June-August 2008 being one of the longest summers of my life. I wanted so badly to begin training players, but the challenge for someone who never ran a business was how to find customers. I remember putting flyers on cars at just about every store in town, putting ads in newspapers, writing coaches at local HS, and even going to local parks trying to find kids and parents to let them know about the training services I would be offering to local youth. Finally securing a few clients was encouraging but with super reasonable prices (almost giving training way) and just a few clients my original business idea was beginning to look more like a hobby instead of a business. Seeing the dramatic changes in the skill sets of the handful players I was working with just added fuel to my desire to actual be a full time trainer. Also now that I had players who were being impacted by the training the thought of not being there for them in the future was tough to accept. At this point in time, I remember asking myself what would I do if I knew I could not fail. Without hesitation, my response to myself was be a basketball skills trainer. I declared to myself at that moment that I will learn everything I need to know, go read books on how to run a business and I was willing to do whatever it took to be successful. Having the desire to do whatever it took was one thing, but the biggest determining factor in how I made it from declaring this training business attempt as a hobby to actually now having trained for 8years was faith. I attribute my longevity to having faith it was going to work even when I couldn't physically see any possible way. Later my faith progressing to I don't have to know how it's going to work but trust that it's going to work and just do my part by putting in the work. I cannot even fathom what my life would have been like had I given up. Not having the impact on both Haley's, Brady, Kimmy, Lexi and Jayla not to mention the thousands of other players who I worked with during my training career. The process of achieving your goals might be filled with uncertainty, doubt, and many struggles but what is most detrimental is you not pursuing who you can become and what you can accomplish if you NEVER GIVE UP. Throughout the entire book, we talked about all the characteristics, behaviors, and mindsets that are a must not only to achieve success but also become a successful person in the process. Never Give Up is the final stage and defining stage. Many will falter or fail because of fatigue, doubt, or focusing on what they don't have, negative self-talk etc. but only Champions refuse to quit no matter how hard it gets. For a Champion, the only option is to achieve desired goals and experience victory. You too can reach the highest pinnacle of success that of becoming a Champion if you declare to NEVER GIVE UP.

BREAK TIME

Step 8: Never Give Up

Reaching your goals and being successful will not come without setback and disappointments, but no matter how difficult it gets you must declare to NEVER GIVE UP!!

It isn't enough just to play the game, your ultimate goal should be to leave your mark and leave a legacy you are proud of. The success you wish to have as opposed to the outcome you will have on the court or in life depends on diligently implementing these behaviors and mindsets to your life:

COURAGE

Have enough Courage to become the best YOU

HEART

Heart and Mind overcome all

ADVERSITY

Must Work through Adversity

MENTALITY

Must think like a Champion to become one

PREPARATION

Preparation+Opportunity=Success

INSPIRATION

Have a mental image of your dreams

OPPORTUNITY

Seize the moment

NEVER GIVE UP

Never give up until you succeed

One thought comes to mind as this book comes to its inevitable end. There is no greater feeling than you becoming who you were created to be. I know who you are. You are a Champion. The book you've just read is just a guide to lay out a pathway showing you how to get from where you are now to where you belong. You have everything you need to elevate yourself to great accomplishments, to maximize your potential. Go for it.

DEVELOPING THE 8 CHARACTERISTICS OF BECOMING A CHAMPION

C - Courage

What does the phrase have the courage to become the best you mean?

_____
_____
_____
_____
_____

Courage Statement:

_____
_____
_____
_____
_____

What steps will you take to become the best you?

_____
_____
_____
_____
_____

H - Heart

What does the phrase Heart and Mind Overcome All mean?

_____
_____
_____
_____

Heart and Mind Overcome All Statement:

_____
_____
_____
_____

How will your Heart and Mind Overcome All statement affect you as a player and person?

_____
_____
_____
_____

A - Adversity

What is Adversity?

_____
_____
_____
_____
_____

Adversity Statement:

_____
_____
_____
_____
_____

How will you overcome adversity as a player and a person?

_____
_____
_____
_____
_____

M - Mentality

What does it mean to think like a CHAMPION?

_____
_____
_____
_____
_____

Champion Statement:

_____
_____
_____
_____
_____

What things will you do daily to become a Champion on and off the court?

_____
_____
_____
_____
_____

P - Preparation

How does Preparation+Opportunity=Success?

Preparation Statement:

What steps will you take to prepare for your success on and off the court?

I - Inspiration

What is inspiration?

_____
_____
_____
_____
_____

What sources will you draw inspiration from to become a Champion?

_____
_____
_____
_____
_____

How will you stay inspired to reach your Goals and Dreams?

_____
_____
_____
_____
_____

O - Opportunity

What opportunities do you have daily to become a better basketball player and person?

_____
_____
_____
_____

Opportunity Statement:

_____
_____
_____
_____

How will you get more out of the opportunities give so you can reach your goals and dreams?

_____
_____
_____
_____

Never Give Up

What does "Never Give up mean to you?

_____
_____
_____
_____
_____

Never Give Up statement:

_____
_____
_____
_____
_____

How will you keep from giving up on your dreams and goals?

_____
_____
_____
_____
_____

Name: _____

Date: ____/____/_____

Developing the 8 characteristics of becoming a Champion

Daily Goals

_____
_____
_____
_____
_____
_____
_____
_____
_____
_____
_____
_____

Action Plan:

_____
_____
_____
_____
_____
_____
_____
_____
_____
_____
_____
_____

Weekly Goals

Action Plan:

1 month goal

Action Plan:

3 month goal

Action Plan:

6 month goal

_____
_____
_____
_____
_____
_____
_____
_____
_____
_____
_____

Action Plan:

_____
_____
_____
_____
_____
_____
_____
_____
_____
_____
_____
_____

9 month goal

Action Plan:

Developing the 8 characteristics of becoming a Champion

1 year goal

Action Plan: